HOLDING PATTERNS
A COLLECTION OF WORDS ON RITUAL

Edited by Beth Brown Ables and Angie Toole Thompson

Editing:
Beth Brown Ables
Angie Toole Thompson

Cover Artwork:
Sallie Harrison

Book Design:
Lib Ramos

Copyright © 2023 Good Printed Things and the individual contributors published within this volume

All rights reserved

First Edition
Printed in the United States of America
goodprintedthings.com
Greenville, South Carolina

ISBN: 978-1-7345844-4-8

HOLDING PATTERNS

a collection of words on ritual

GOOD PRINTED THINGS

INTRODUCTION

I lit a brand new candle the other day. Struck a match, stood in brief admiration and then, as with most novelties, I just let it burn. In fact, I forgot about it entirely. That candle burned all night and well into the next day until my faulty, old porch door flung open from a wayward breeze and the flame died.

My house, once bathed with amber and vetiver and whatever other smells make a space feel grounded and whole, now hazed with a thin and final strand of smoke.

Ritual is like this for me. I know it mostly by its absence. Only when my ratted and defaced black Chuck Taylors went missing in 2006 could I see them for the sacred footwear they were to me. Only when we moved houses could I identify a simple walk in my old neighborhood as a spiritual practice. Only when I miss three little blue pills in a row do I feel the darkness of depression reenter my orbit and validate their power.

I admire those who keep their rituals close – naming them, building their days around them, defining their forms. This practice begets a strong mind and family traditions and even national holidays.

While I aspire to more meaningfully ordered days (and fewer forgotten meds), I'll just light another candle, feel the atmosphere shift, and let it burn.

ANGIE TOOLE THOMPSON

PART

Routine

You wake up and your horoscope says you will put on your shoes, so you do. You stand in line for coffee like it is your job and destiny, and when the barista hands you a latte that is absolutely not what you ordered, you raise it to your lips and see what acceptance tastes like. You wait for the crossing light, and remember your college girlfriend who was stopped for jaywalking so many times by the campus cop that she was called into the Dean's office for it. Her name was Amanda, and her hair was red. You had a sneaking suspicion that she was too good for you, and so before graduation, before she could ask you to move to New York with her, you told her she was too much. Too wild. Too unpredictable. You heard from another alum that Amanda finally broke into Broadway, and that critics rave about her presence and energy. You even looked up her IMDB last night in bed, waiting for the tidal wave of regret to subsume your weary body. But then the app on your phone that regulates such things told you it was time to go to sleep, so you did.

Good Morning, Moons

a father puts his children to bed.
"good night, loves," he says
before turning out the lamplight
to reveal the moons' steady gaze.

at daybreak his children wake early
and hide unseen behind the drapes.
"good morning, loves," he says
to the titter of windowpanes.

beyond them, even the sky
has forgotten the moons:
their glowing faces overshadowed
by brighter objects.

The Earth Is Tender Now

We can say at least the grass was mowed,
and dogs allowed off leash careened
towards frisbee orbs, cherry trees held

their petals as long as one does. We can
say at least we were happy
at cards around the kitchen table,

sunsets were pink and turned
the trees' new leaves neon,
and oceans stayed mostly

within their shores. We can say
at least the earth kept its tilt
and the child her spunk and the cat

its midnight prowl. We can say at least
the hours were 60 minutes and even
though cars didn't leave their spots

we washed the pollen off, and we
wiped down doorknobs with bleach,
and we worried the fringes of throw blankets.

We can say at least that we tried not to
cry, and we kept laughing, and we can say
somehow at least we lived.

"so even if spring continues to disappoint / we can say at least the lettuce loved the rain" is from "Dear One Absent This Long While" by Lisa Olstein

Apple Pie

What I meant to say was I would love a slice of your apple pie. I never told you that my mother made apple pie every Easter, but we only ate it after she'd dragged us to the west-side catholic church with stained glass set afire in tangerine and sapphire, and made us pray to God and ask forgiveness for never praying, never giving thanks, even though we never went to church any other day of the year. That's a God damn good pie, she'd say, and I'd fill my mouth with its soft-baked insides heavy with brown sugar and melting granny smiths.

What I meant to say was I like your apple pie better, because the crust is crisp, so crisp I know you brushed it in yolk like you do sometimes; delicately brushed, just like your last painting, taking your time with one layer after another of ochre oil paint with its strange, nutty fragrance. Your apple pies are a combination of spice and lemon-tart that is particularly yours and some days, they smell just like home. Your pie is not earned, it is not solace; it's too-hot slices eaten at any time of day. It waits for me to slice it open. The pie's steam licks the air in tendrils on the kitchen counter. I can eat it, I can weep, I can walk out the door with a slice in my hand and wander the path through the park I've been meaning to walk, alone. You return to find me sitting in the dark; the winter night fell early and my slice is half-eaten and cold. No, it's not a bother, when you turn on the light, when you breathe down the back of my neck, mouth gurgling with pools of affection. Even though I tense, waiting for the heavier boot that will never fall.

What I meant to say was I'm grateful you always try, even when I don't. Perhaps I do try, I try with such an effort I inevitably find myself in the depths of a labyrinth. I'm grateful you're not like me, not like *her*, that you're your own person, with a quick and uncanny sense of measurement and an energetic desire to see the world through its everyday veneer. I'm jealous of you, the way you hug me firmly, low-pitched gurgles audible in your belly when you squeeze me without restraint. Jealous of the way you open the half-broken latch of the kitchen window to smell the damp freshness of the mornings.

What I meant to say was, yes, I'll unzip from the tight, geometric routine I have woven around myself and eat that slice of pie. Notch by notch, my skin catching. My tongue, far-away from me, tastes the sweetness. I'll even go to church with you, the church down the street with the dark stained glass and lingering scent of smoke. Incense and cold-stone and ritual bring me back to myself, to you. I'll even linger in our church, the one you joke is made up of our bed, the altar. Yes, I'll try and notice the morning sun signaling yet another glorious day. Sure, I see it now, the yellow light through our warped glass window, swirling across the clean bedspread, and you, haloed.

Scheduled Downtime

I used to have a crying appointment
Every Saturday 8:30 AM
Back when I was five
Too young to know
Too proud to ask
Why the entire school assembly–
Juniors, seniors, teachers alike
Crooned my name for a whole five minutes
"Vishaal…overcome!, Vishaal…overcome!
Sooooomedayyyy eh, eh?"
Now, what–

what'd I done this time?
I'd hang my head in shame,
Wipe my tears with the handkerchief my mother pinned to my shirt
Waiting for the someday I'd be too old for a mass reprimand
And now when I look back,

Three decades hence

Too old for a pinned handkerchief (and supposedly, a mother)

Too proud to ask

As the appointments come and go as they please

And no one bothered if I succumb

I'd take that Saturday back in a heartbeat.

O Lilac

After "Lilacs for Voice & Orchestra" composed by George Walker in response to "When Lilacs Last in the Dooryard Bloom'd" by Walt Whitman

The lilac bush at the back of my childhood home—
the old-fashioned kind, high as the brown

roof, heart leaves, sick-sweet blooms whose May stems
I would bundle with wet paper towel and aluminum

foil, to bring to school and lay at the feet of the statue
of the Virgin Mary—queen of May. As children we do

these things—gesture and custom as adults tell us,
costume ourselves, sadden ourselves at deaths,

assuming adults know what they're doing. Grown, we decide
how to mourn the deaths of fathers, sisters, lovers—like

Hindus on riverbanks, like Whitman mourned Lincoln,
like encircled elephants, swaying. How old was I when

my parents' gods stopped reigning over me, my parents'
ballots no longer biblical, their radio prophets selling

souls I refused to buy? I know how my mother would
prefer I mourn her someday—with tight jaw, fried

perch, passed-around photos, and recorded instrumental
music. Flowers? I suppose. Tulips or something else

cut from the yard. No politics talk at the cake and coffee.
As a child it never occurred to me that we

can carve our own statues, Decide who to pray for,
to pray to, at whose feet to place flowers.

The World and I converse.

Maiden World.
A sunrise artist, fresh dew
finger painting
black roses in Halfeti-
Avant - garde.

The World,
A Mother / Noon
tends to wounds.
And I too,
sit with scars.

I run my fingers
along old stitches
caress their pale snaking
and think of ink,
and of my ancestors.

Gathering little fragments,
mementos of this journey.
Flowers, feathers
  beads,
and stones.

In my *becoming*,
I turn my insides
  out.
Shrouding myself
as an altar.

Lighting the wick of sundown,
the Crone
in silver majesty.
She sings of Black roses blooming Halfeti,
of Enki filling Euphrates with desire.

At the end of every Sunday School class

we have orange juice or Tang and doughnuts, day
-old but still delish and I think we eat
in remembrance of me like Jesus said
to the disciples, the Big 12, so that
the juice is like blood and the pastry is
the body, if doughnuts are pastry, and
if not they're near enough, like poetry
or a cartoon Superman instead of
the real thing, forget that there isn't one
but anyway then we all pray and of
course we prayed before we ate and I pray
harder when there's real juice instead of fake
which I can get at home anyhow and
for doughnuts only oatmeal. But no holes.

Encores

The concert is over
the band has left the stage
the lights remain down, though
for the best bit to play out:
the cries of 'We love you!'
the rapturous applause
the whistles and catcalls
and stomping for more;
it's savage and synchronised
a battle most joyous
to woo and to wear down
and bring the band back
for one more—that's the game;
we know how it ends
but still we're not certain;
the thrill's in the timing, the tension
and if once, then why not once more?
the cycle repeats and it's boots to the floor;
yes, we're under a highly prized, ritualised spell
a moment in memory, unscripted, inevitable
never quite the same, this wild ruckus
and yet, seldom much different—
such comfort from cacophonous wellsprings;
they're coming back!
this, most of all, is what I love

Or, so it was, in those evening of yore;
now bands leave the stage and reclaim it
through a fast-revolving door—
You've been wonderful! Thank you, good night!
means: brace for the end, the cut-off is inviolable;
don't get your hopes up;
the let-down's a red line on the set list;
we'll come back, sing 'Gentlemen, time!'
and then see ourselves out;
no clapping, no hope for revival;
the lights come up;
clinical, soulless;
goodbye

I don't like it; it lacks that key spark—
just a pattern, a programme
like shouting out 'Taxi!' at a restaurant
when someone breaks a glass;
just a Simon Says reflex, entrenched;
not a play, to and fro, to be savoured and shared;
no, the encore is gone—it's a ghost without spirit
but it lingers inside us, waiting, reminding
that we make our own rituals, free from the rut
in the way we respond whenever we're wooed
and inveigled: don't go through the motions;
be the band! keep the world guessing—
will they or won't they?
until the end

The Women Who Walk Before Me

I walk over broken bits of shells
looking for whole ones that remind me of my mother.
The women in my family share two things—
a collection of shells,
and a history of divorce.

My shadow walks beside me and I think
of the miles those women have trudged,
bent and broken on a beach,
searching for something.

I bend beside their ghosts,
one of them pointing to a shell
that makes me believe in mermaids,
another holding out an
octopus tentacle of coral.

My grandmother's ghost hands me a black rock
that, if you haven't given up dreaming
and if close your eyes,
could be a shark's tooth.

I walk and I drop them all with a plink
down into the cup I carry
where they nestle
among the words I've been collecting:

Debris and penance.
Insatiable, wrath.
Solace and surrender.

They've begun haunting me
like the women who walk before me,
eyes down, feet slow—
half a dozen divorces and
a handful of shells between us.

Rituals

On Fridays we make Palomas with the rosemary by the mailbox. We let our grinning children harvest too much but still wink a thank you. Their dirty hands earthy from the herbs. I can't help but inhale them, cupped to my face, before I scrub them clean. On Sundays my parents and grandparents come over for coffee, and hopefully a dessert my mother made "just in case." My Papa always brings his great grandchildren Baby Ruth's candy bars and they squeal before he is even in the door. I chase them around the kitchen to wipe their sticky hands. They groan and giggle while I try to hold the fleeting moment by its wings - four generations strong, crammed around our creaking wooden table. Each December we are blanketed by the scent of dried orange slices while we make misshapen cookies and call them perfect. We share them with our neighbor. We forget to make Christmas cards but vow that next year will be our year. Year after year, a drowsy newborn baby, swaddled in thin muslin hope, laid in the same woven bassinet. Each one insisting on outgrowing it too fast, too soon. Each time we swear, "this is the last one." Each time we are glad to have been wrong.

Ode to an Assistant

Hi,

I hope this poem finds you well
circling back here re:
your bruised spirit
checking in to see if you can
make it
through to 6, no, 7, no, 8, no
EOD
when your boss has left the building
and you're left with a to-do list like a sourdough starter which
left unchecked will grow and grow, so
you tear off chunks and use it to make art
to make sustenance
to make something beautiful
for someone else.
Who needs it! Don't get me wrong,
and this whole thing you're doing, you need it too,
or at least that's what they all say
It's one year, roughly
which will weed out those without the will
and the drive to survive in this business and
you're nothing if not driven!
That's why you drive forty five minutes on the 10 going there,
an hour and ten coming back where
you're a drop in a river and
for some reason, no one is ever in a rush to get back home...

But you know why, it's
because everything that matters is on your desk
is in your inbox
is in a calendar invite you forgot to send out—
fuck! Okay, mental note. Send invites to
Steve, Jean, Kathleen, Lydia, Mike,
Jesus Christ
will a break ever come?
Please let me know when you get the chance!
In the meantime, you're
climbing the rungs of a ladder, unsung
maybe after this year you'll make a lateral
move to CAA? To UTA? your friend at Eva Longoria's company is
sitting in on development meetings
fuck her
I mean, good for her
really, you wish the best for her
but if you just had that taste
that time and space, in a room
that would make it all worth it
and then you can actually mean it when you say
Best,

Anyways,
I mean it when I say
it isn't all a waste.
And just in case you won't hear it today,
Thank you.

Mother Mornings

Tired woman, wake
Before the lights. Hear
The reverb of your silent
Prayer-hopes catching wind
And echoing throughout your home.
Penetrating doors, permeating rooms.
Peace, dusting square feet
Like dew on the new day grass.

When you sleep, the same
Things happen. Your rest
Billows out and blankets
Snoozing bodies, dreaming
In their beds. I read a book
That says those
Who plan peace, prosper.
And so,
I plan to prosper in this peace.

Woman Hands

I watched her making yucca rope with her hands.
Tugging apart thick strands of nature
Into frayed strips of green. Ends
Tied to the porch posts. Fingers forming braids
Back and forth, binding each strand to the other.

There is something about woman hands.
How they twist and toil and make things
That endure. But also, the things they do that become
Things undone by nightfall, over and over and over.

Gumball Machine

The gumball machine always sat in the corner, tucked behind the swinging door and the crowds that often awaited their tables. Perhaps no one paid it as much attention as I frequently did. There would always be a little flutter of excitement, searching to find a quarter nearby. And then, like clockwork, a quarter I would find. I'd place it in the coin slot and listen intently as the gears turned. *Give me a blue,* I'd think to myself. *Oh please, give me a blue.* I'd crouch down, still full of excitement–waiting and watching. A yellow gumball would spiral down and my smile would fade. It was alright. Not what I wanted, falling short of my expectations–but it was alright.

Maybe a blue will come next. Papa would laugh as I'd approach him for another quarter. I'd try again. I'd listen as the gears turned. *Give me a blue,* I'd think. *Oh please, give me a blue.* I'd hold onto my hope, but my smile would fade yet again as I watched a pink gumball make its way down to my hand. Pink was alright. Not great. But it was alright.

It'd happen again, a repeated cycle–a dance between me and the gumball machine that'd never seem to end. I slowly realized that no matter how badly I wanted a blue gumball, nothing was guaranteed. I'd use every quarter in sight and be disappointed with a handful of pieces I never wanted in the first place. I'd force a smile and fake some joy. *Look at all I've gotten,* I'd say with a false sense of pride. What did I even have to prove, to enjoy? I'd used up all I had and gotten nothing in return. It was enough to fake some satisfaction - but not enough to fulfill.

He'd been my gumball machine.

Give me a blue, I'd think to myself. *Oh please, give me a blue.*

But–just like the disappointing handful of colors–I'd always be left grasping for more. I'd love with all I had and all I was, searching intently for more and more to offer in hopes that one day my hopes and dreams would be met. I'd hope that it was just a matter of sorting through the disappointments before the long awaited blue gumball would drop.

I love you, I'd say. In goes the quarter. *I know,* he'd reply. Out comes the yellow.

I need you, I'd plead. In goes the quarter. *You're fine,* he'd reply. Out comes the pink.

I want you, I'd beg. In goes the quarter. *Whatever,* he'd reply. Out comes the red.

In went the quarters—time and time again—but the blue never came.

The Bed is My Altar

I nestle sheepishly towards
Bed. Aren't we all a bit of being
embarrassed when we face
salvation? I mean, the alluring
rustle of sheets is the feel
of heaven, manifold.

The body glides through
the soft and silent surface that
manifests what peace means;
Like the nail on the cross,
the body impales

The hands, they grasp the
pillow like a body, or a bread.
How so? You are not capable
of salvation. The world is unfair
that is why the hands, they affix
into a prayer, proper and in position
For some salvation, or just an exposition.

But like love, they would break
again. For they forget the covers
that would envelop their sin. This
Body would be covered with linen
like a corpse. But the difference is
it would not take me three days
to rise again.

Devotion

At my grandmother's house sits a shrine to our ancestor. Every morning, my grandmother kneels and prays. She closes her eyes and hums tunelessly lighting sticks of incense. The air fills with their heady scent. I don't know what she asks our ancestors for, but since she began this daily ritual there has been a change in her – she – a harvest moon carving its boon alongside a pearled sky. And whenever I visit home for *Tet* or our ancestor's death anniversary. I kneel and pray too. I hold the incense and close my eyes. And for a few moments I am weightless.

new omens

these are the ways i count myself lucky:

waking before the alarm
no bills in the mailbox

these are the ways i know i am not:

"case still pending"
"more tests required"

i tell myself i am flexible, adaptive:

a cup of broken needles, kept,
open and close the same app three times

but i am still looking for signs:

new growth on dormant houseplant
the finding of postage stamps

Casting Runes

these marks upon my arms
are not for charms or meant
to be charming, they are not
for protection, not for kurt
cobain, and though i like it
when a friend asks if this
one on my left hand is a *dandelion
seed*, it is not a symbol for that
either. these are a *bridge* to
the other side i could never
reach wherever i traveled or
what languages i learned to speak,
they are in *honor* of my sitti
and in *defiance* of my family,
they are a duty paid *to tradition*
and a two finger salute to
the policing of tradition. may
these signs on my hands make
me legible as *bad* other, *dangerous* other, yes a *real* mother, a spell
cast against ever backing
down or trying to hide, these are
wards cast against passing for
someone more assimilated or
well-behaved. no i will not *tell*
you what they mean   they mean
everything, they remember me
to *mystery* and every *story* my
grandmother never told me
and every *origin* story my
father never told me and every
inkwell to write my own story
that my family never wanted
for me, and so i wrote them
all here on my hands right at
the *fat* hinge-joints where
I hook my thumbs into the
wheel of the world and turn.

Pill Box

I've learned to carry with me a small pill box every day. You see, I have a series of maladies.

I have an illness in speaking with strangers. I want to appear to them as the best human they have ever met. Or at least, I hope that they will forget me.

I may never see them again, but I worry myself sick over their unknowable thoughts. When I am checking out at the grocery store I will silently catch the clerk's eyes and suddenly wonder, "Does she like me? Is she impressed with my good-natured comments about the day? Does she feel like I'm a real human girl?"

So, I've learned when I see the clerk waiting, it is best if I reach into my box to take a pill.

I have another worser condition. A sickness with people I already know. The problem here is that of familiarity. We have a history together. They have a frame of reference. I cringe when I feel these friends and acquaintances draw near. I assume that each moment I speak with them that I am either improving my image in their eyes or I am slightly degrading it. I'm rising or falling. Always. If I rose the last time we talked, I hope to go months before seeing them again so as not to chance another encounter. I want to leave them impressed. And then never need to see them again.

I try to avoid these discussions whenever possible. Sometimes I go the long way round the building or take the hallway on the floor below.

When I cannot avoid them I reach into my box for a pill.

Perhaps the most difficult moments are the times when I am with myself. I dislike myself intensely. I fear myself because I know me extremely well. I know everything I have ever been frightened of and every awful thing I have done or thought. I know all my weaknesses and I exploit this knowledge mercilessly against me to my advantage. I accuse myself repeatedly. I take delight in wallowing in my own wretched failure. You might think that I should be sympathetic to myself and willing to help. Perhaps I should see myself as a needy orphan. Why can't I swoop in to rescue myself? No. I throw the self-inflicted darts the hardest.

The only thing that helps me in these moments with myself is to take a pill.

See now, let me show you my pill box. I'll open it for you so that you can peer inside. Ah, you've noticed…it is empty. There are no pills. Yet reaching for it is the only way to survive the fear.

What is the fear, you might wonder? It is the memory of what I used to use to coat my days. The mornings were aching and dry and my mind didn't fully feel like my own until I could drink. I could mentally map out the course of each day drink by drink. I would name the drinks. This one is "Medicine." The next one is "Morning." The next…"Afternoon"… and "Evening," and "Bedtime"…and there were ones sprinkled in between like "Unexpected Socializing" or "Booster Shot" or "Normal Face." There were, truthfully, too many too name. But they are what I used before I had a pill box.

Today there are no more drinks. Instead there is a white page…a just-raised pencil…a determined twist of the lips. There is an empty pill box which I reach for every day.

Ritual; burned

Begin your day by taking a piece of aloe between your fingers
and crushing it. Feel the cool substance
leak from between,

Raise it to your mouth
and touch a thorn with your tongue.

Listen to the sound the aloe makes
as you crush it,
smear it between your fingers.

Rub it over your heart
and dig deep into the potting soil.

Remember to smell the air from the window,
and taste it as well.

Whatever you hear outside,
that is the music of the work you make
from sinew and sap.

Taste of Memory

It feels like time travel, but it isn't.

Paula wakes up around six. She needs an hour to herself, to shower, meditate, eat her oatmeal with raspberries and cream. Then she braids her long auburn hair and puts on the caregiver's uniform. Technically, it's cheating, but every other option has proven to be more agitating for Henry.

His room is a lie. It looks like a normal bedroom: white oak furniture, elegant grey walls and a large window overlooking the facility lawn, but in reality, it hides a system monitoring his brain waves, controlling his sleep, regulating his vital functions.

Henry's sleep is medicated – waking up in the middle of the night would be extremely dangerous. His face is smooth, untroubled. She bends down and kisses his lips lightly: it might be the only kiss she'll get that day.

It's seven o'clock on a winter morning and the window displays a white fog rolling over the lawn, diffusing the weak silvery light. Henry shuffles in his sleep, mumbles something intelligible. Paula sits beside the bed and braces herself.

He opens his eyes, grey as the morning outside, and Paula sees the usual sequence of emotions in them: confusion, fear, panic.

"Where am I?" He sits up, pulls the monitor's headband off his head. "What is this?"

Paula gives him a calm, professional smile. Everything else, any display of emotion, would push him into a frenzy, and the day would spiral into irreparable mess.

"You had an accident," she says. "You've suffered memory loss, but you don't have any other injuries."

"Oh." He takes a minute to process that.

Paula's eyes are glued to his face, she never gets tired of its clear planes and sharp shadows. If she's careful and lucky, by the end of the day, he'll let her touch him. Not yet, though. There's the whole introduction dance they have to go through first.

"Who am I?" he asks at last.

The same question every morning.

"You're Henry Wheeler, thirty-nine years old. You slipped on the ice in front of your house," she says. It's so banal it's almost funny: one wrong step and your whole life is erased.

"I don't remember it," he says, and his eyes glaze over for a moment, as he searches for any sliver of information to hold on to. But there's nothing, there never is. "And who are you?"

"I'm Paula, your caregiver." The lie slips easily off her tongue after so much practice.

"Is this a hospital?" His gaze examines the stylish furniture.

"An assisted living facility for memory recovery," she says. "Don't worry if you can't remember anything now. It's normal after such an injury. The memory will start trickling back in no time."

Henry smiles and it breaks her heart. It's been three years and it hasn't come back. Every morning, his memory is a clean slate.

They cried so much over it in the first months. Paula showed him their wedding photos, love letters, souvenirs from their travels. His famous blog, his brilliant restaurant reviews. He raved and cried and blamed himself. "I'll remember tomorrow," he swore. "I will."

But there is no tomorrow for him. Only today, over and over again.

"Are you hungry?" she chirps, cutting off dark thoughts. "I can fix you some breakfast and then we can talk."

"Sure." He's always ravenous in the morning.

She has a fully equipped kitchen and a well-stocked fridge; she cooks for him every day. It makes her feel useful. The food builds a bridge between them when words fail.

Today's breakfast is a crusty ciabatta with creamy butter, prosciutto, provolone and lamb's lettuce. They ate it on their honeymoon in Italy, on a sunny terrace with wrought-iron chairs and round tables.

He emerges from the bathroom wearing dark slacks and a blue shirt, his fair hair still wet from the shower.

"Try this," she pushes the plate towards him.

Watching his face as he takes a bite is the first high of her day.

"This is delicious," he says.

His memory might have been erased, but his instincts are intact. He's always loved her food. His review of her restaurant, a lifetime ago, opened the door for her first Michelin star. He's been her greatest fan and her most meticulous critic.

He still is.

"Verona," he suddenly says. "Caffe Al Teatro."

She freezes.

He stares at his sandwich, then at his hands. "How long have I been here?"

He's never asked that question before. "L-long enough," she stammers.

"My hands look different," he whispers. "Where's my wedding ring?"

Hope pierces her heart like an arrow. "Henry?"

He lifts his head and there's a spark in his eyes she hasn't seen for years. "I know you," he says, breathing hard.

She blinks away the tears and holds her tongue, afraid that she might ruin everything.

"Paula?" he says, eyes glued to her face. "Paulina, my love, what happened to me?"

END

Compulsions

*The things you
worry about
never happen.*
Challenge accepted.
I string my worries like beads,
count them off
like some frantic rosary,
turn them into routine.
Small and large
jumble together
until they become
indistinguishable,
a never-ending loop of
destruction,
death,
doom.
I let each one absorb
my fingerprints,
try to remind it
who's in control
even as I add
countless more.
The string of them
wraps around
and around my body,
squeezing tighter
and tighter,
and though I long
to break free,
suppose this is
the only thing
keeping me together?
A new worry.
I begin the count
again.

Body Math

Start always with the heart and the lungs
Engine and bellows
Run yourself back to the amniotic beat
and then that first great grasping of air

> *Always back, selah*

A given Tuesday or Thursday of any given month
    in any given year
Count the laps
Match to heartbeat
Match to tracheal rhythm
The count, the interval
(Root of "ritual" may be "to count,"
    "to observe closely")
200 meters, 35 seconds
check check
time embeds in your flesh
touch the starting line
listen for the bell
alveoli talk to capillaries
count the pulse
match again to round and rhythm
hit the line
start again
and again

    again

> *breathe out, and don't lose your watch*

the long lope,
the telling of circuits,
your own rosalium,
marked by a hill you have carried hundreds of times,
    by a bridge you have criss-crossed hundreds of times
tap the brick as you pass that wall
nod to the rose-bush at the crossroad
10 miles in 80 minutes
ventricular chant
tarry not and never deviate,
oh no, don't change the route
check check
10 Ks in 45 minutes
greet each checkpoint and touchstone
honor your tutelaries
and they will honor you

    breathe in, and where is your watch?

beats, beats, beats per minute
time infuses your kidneys, your liver, the
    core indeed
measured in prescribed metrics, intervals, increments
check the count
no change in the count
on any given Tuesday

end always with the lungs and the heart
emulate your first great race
daily rites to inscribe in the body
the endless memory of your first ritual
a marathon, not a sprint

    Always back, selah.

Morning Dreams
There used to be
Some sort of repeating theme
Where I would arrive
After I was meant to

An enduring struggle
Tooth and nail
To reach
.
The sun became
An interruption

What kind of feeling
Except a pause
Between knowing
        And known
Something there that has left
With a tense goodbye

What kind of feeling
When you fall
Pushing through the screen
But I pulled you back
We laugh together

What kind of feeling
Looking across
Small letters
That curved impossibly
As I memorize the shape
With the pad of my thumb

What kind of feeling
So I call
To listen

Sometimes, I am still
in the morning
when the light comes
peeking through blinds
with just the right angle

Before the sound rushes in
And I taste words
early under my tongue
I lay there, glancing
at the alarm clock
wishing for five more

I tap turn mumble
Refusing to settle

Because

Only sometimes I am still
In-between moments
Tangled in the day

Walking the Yard

I usually begin a new bed or border by thinking about where to plant. I try to know how much sun shines on that spot and gauge the soil quality. I select plants that are well suited for Minnesota, able to withstand our possible temperature extremes. But other design decisions seem much more fun. Will plants grow vertically? Do I value statuary? If so, are we talking Grecian urns or giant ladybugs? Who knew concrete blocks could be stacked and painted to create pyramids for succulents? Pinterest distracts me from the big picture: what Alexander Pope, borrowing from the ancient Egyptian concept of "genius loci," called the "spirit of the place." That means planting gardens that honor the place itself, thinking about how this garden affects the host environment, as well as how it will serve as habitat. Gardeners need to recognize the plants, animals, and insects that share space. We need knowledge. We start by paying attention to the world around us.

**

Every spring, as soon as a hint of anything green pokes through the melting snow, I walk the yard. I stare intently at the ground, my head cocked slightly, and I circle the house, usually first thing in the morning. I walk from flower bed to flower bed, trying to locate and identify plants as they wake from winter sleep. In the early weeks of the season, gardeners crave time with plants, those they've known for decades and newer acquaintances—which they may not remember planting. I walk the yard to bring them back. Each step echoes below the earth like a heartbeat until my body itself begins to remember. My lips turn up as I stare at the space south of the honey locust, even before I recognize the emotion: joy. This must be where I planted tulips—probably the ivory ones. My eyes widen and my chest rises with a quick breath as my body signals wonder. Aha. Balloon flower. My nostrils flare in mild annoyance as I stare down at what must be the deadnettle. The foliage is gorgeous but deadnettle spreads everywhere.

As I walk the yard, I see and acknowledge each plant. I take photographs in my mind. Sometimes I title photos as I go: *Still Life of Lily with Gravel; Lily Between Phlox and Daisy*. Many gardeners do this—at least, the walking part—in early spring, eager to know which plants reseed themselves, what's already germinated, what has failed to grow. Then in October, just before the first predicted frost, I scan the garden beds with new urgency. I tell myself, *don't forget what's here*. But when winter arrives, the snow covers last season's garden stories like Liquid Paper, whiting everything out until I can no longer discern what lies below.

**

I wonder what pediatricians see when they examine a child? I once saw some stranger staring at my anxious kid, naked and vulnerable beneath a paper gown. Luckily, we eventually found a great pediatrician. He identifies as a person with ADD and one of his grandsons is on the spectrum. He talks openly about how he learned to live with ADD when he meets with my sons. I can remember many visits where he spent more than 30-40 minutes with us. My sons tell me now how much they always appreciated that. I appreciated it, too. But it's depressing that we view this pediatrician–his attention to his patients and his very existence–extraordinary.

So many stories begin with an encounter between a stranger and one of my children. One pair of eyes stares intently at one of my three sons, observing, noticing, searching for ways that he deviates from expectations. My middle child, Ellet, was the first to be noticed this way; as a toddler, his daycare teachers expressed concerns. These teachers spent 30-40 hours with him each week, watching and learning. We trusted these eyes. We listened to their suggestions, consulted experts.

**

When I walk the yard, I always begin at our front door, which faces west. I descend three steps, turn sharply to the left and travel south, following the walkway that forms a concrete boundary between the two main flower beds in the front yard. The first, the large oval between the front steps and the driveway, is closest to the house. On the walkway's other side, a narrow, curving bed snakes along the entire length of concrete. I keep the house on my left as I first move towards the driveway, inspecting the narrow bed to my right. I love this bed best in early summer, before the day lilies open. The space is filled with pinks and purples: wild geranium, a Blue Angel clematis, and pink candytuft. By the end of summer, though, the morning glories take over.

Once I reach the driveway, I turn around and head back toward the front door to check the bed closest to the house. In 2005, I scattered an entire box of shade tolerant wildflower seed, plus a small packet of mixed sun loving perennial seed for good measure. I bought them both for under five bucks from Arrow Ace Hardware. Back then, a tight cluster of three silver birch trees near the driveway and a giant honey locust at the other end of the yard shaded the front of the house, but I figured it couldn't hurt to spread both kinds of wildflower seeds.

Good call. The birches came down after a vicious storm a few years later, so the area was sunnier for a quite a while. Now, a new trio of birch trees grows from the same spot. Candytuft, tickseed, sweet William and daisies all grow in abundance there, mostly descendants of those first scattered seeds. There's also Russian sage, Asiatic lilies, and morning glories. Even my favorite shade-lover, a variegated Jacob's Ladder with the most gorgeous cream and green striped foliage, keeps thriving even after its environment changed so radically. For the first three years, I had no idea that the Jacob's Ladder could flower. Then, one spring morning, there they were: tiny, delicate bell-shaped blossoms in clusters, all tinted where lavender meets coneflower blue. "Sleep, creep, leap!" gardeners say. It takes three seasons to learn what's really possible for perennials.

**

When a report indicates that Ellet, just shy of 34 months of age, has the general development of a 29-month old, we learn the names and functions of tests and we, too, offer our input. There's the Mullen Scales of Early Learning, the BASC-2, the Adaptive Behavior Assessment System, Ages and States Questionnaire, Peabody Motor, the Infant/Toddler Sensory Profile Questionnaire, Child Development Inventory, the ADOS (Asperger Syndrome Diagnostic Scale). Observations take place May 6, May 13, May 18, and May 19 of 2005. As we read the final report, words blend into toxic soup:

> ...difficulty processing sensory information...escape from noisy environments...agitation when having hair washed...intense seeking out of movement...limited food choices/preferences...dislikes or avoids coloring/drawing...appears stiff, awkward or clumsy...difficulty with bilateral tasks such as fasteners (buttons, zippers)...in constant motion... difficulty sitting still...noted to fall frequently...poor balance skills... difficult to understand when he speaks...easily distracted by sounds... easily frustrated...difficulty getting along with other children...tends to withdraw from groups...

We turn to narrative summaries, puzzled by the numeric values, only to find contradictions among the clinical observations: one observer notes that Ellet was eager to please and enjoys individual attention. Another professional states that during observations of play, Ellet preferred to play alone.

**

The front beds on both sides of the walkway always fill with flowers, but some years a particular color dominates. A cool spring favors the most exquisite cornflower blue flax; a warmer than usual June shines with yellow tickseed. After the birch came down, I added a single shasta daisy plant, assuming I'd need more sun lovers to replace the shady plants that would surely die. But instead of dying, shady perennials just made room for the daisies, which thanked their hosts by reseeding and spreading uncontrollably. I don't care. When daisies prepare to bloom, their tightly knotted petals look like fingers intertwined, pressed against eyes squeezed shut, as if they, too, wait to see what will bloom next, so we can all remove our hands from our faces, open our eyes, and yell, "surprise!"

**

I like to think that walking the yard may be teaching me patience, since growing things rewards me with incremental changes, so small that they are almost imperceptible day to day, but yet month by month, year by year, plants bloom, thrive, produce new seedlings, spread, and change the landscape. Sometimes I pretend I'm walking the yard because I need to water the plants; sometimes I tell myself that I'm there to weed. Walking the yard is the first thing I think of when I wake up in the morning. It's the last thing I do before I shut the house down for the night. Some evenings I'm in the yard so late, I don't even kiss my youngest son, Cyrus—the only one that still tolerates kisses—goodnight.

I use chunks of broken pottery as borders for my beds. No black plastic edging. I love the look of pottery poking from the dirt, and there's always some on hand at the house. The older my kids get, the more I crave the satisfaction of throwing ceramic pots and broken plates to the ground, where they shatter into shards.

I take risks. I sometimes dig a hole and plant something right in the middle of the day, rather than waiting for cooler evening temperatures. I forget to water. I don't use fertilizer of any kind. Still, the plants persist. Perhaps gardeners assume they have more control over what grows than we really do. The cultivated purple coneflower is not so far removed from its wild prairie ancestors.

**

I don't call myself an environmentalist, but I believe that people can and must take responsibility for whatever they grow, wherever they grow it. Environmentalists write urgently about farming practices, chemicals, and climate change. They consider global implications: Climate refugees. Water shortages. Contamination. I write about the natural world in a decidedly local way. I'm a transplanted southerner, fascinated by the incremental changes I see in my own rural Minnesota backyard: those I observe in my plants, and the ones I see in my children. This, I now understand, is a kind of phenology, what naturalist Jim Gilbert describes as "simply observing the natural world and keeping a record of it."[1] I'm only beginning to see how my family's well being mirrors the health of the world outside. Or, maybe it's even more than that. Maybe creating some sort of familial phenology shows me that there is no separation between the so-called "natural world" and my family. Or there shouldn't be. As Gilbert explains, "In this beautiful world of ours, nothing exists on its own."

**

The first child with autism I ever knew was my ex-husband's niece. Diagnosed as a toddler, she was a tiny, thin, delicate little girl with lush curly hair and beautiful green eyes. Her love for junk food was legendary. "Oooh! Wonderful chips," she'd coo when my sister-in-law gave her a small plastic bowl filled with salty potato chips. She also adored Barbie dolls and doomed superstar Selena Quintanilla. She would spend hours in her bedroom as a child, watching the 1997 biopic based on Selena's life, moving her Barbie to match Jennifer Lopez's signature moves. Much of her verbal communication then was echolalia—repeated phrases from television commercials, films, conversations she'd had in the past. But we always sensed that she loved us both. The divorce ended my relationship with her, her older sister, and their mom and grandma.

On the other side of the family tree, my nephew, the oldest of my brother's two sons, now 24 years old and finishing up graduate school, was the first grandchild to be diagnosed with ASD. Between the ages of three and four, he would walk along his house, room to room, always trailing the fingers of his hand along the wall. He seemed to like the reassurance: something was, in fact, next to him, something that always stood still. He'd get this mischievous little half-smile on his face, as if he knew a secret that nobody else shared. Now I imagine how alike we must seem, my nephew and I, as I walk the yard, starting always with the front, making sure to keep the sidewalk on my left side, permitting myself to go to the backyard only after I have traversed the front walkway twice— once on the way to the driveway, and once on the way back. Then I can continue on my quest to walk the whole perimeter of the house.

**

The shrinking area of gravel to the right of my front door teems with lilies of the valley. Here, the house's first owners started a triangle-shaped cluster, but these lovely flowers spread aggressively in the shade.

The summer before my second wedding, I would gather them into a bouquet and stand in front of the mirror, practicing. I always step over the lilies extra carefully as I turn toward the north side of the house. Honoring those lilies of the valley preserves not just the plants but the memories of a fleetingly peaceful time in my life, when my two children spent Sundays with their father, while I devoted the time to Brian, a man I was teenager-crazy in love with. These lilies will soon overtake the entire area, despite the gravel, but I don't care. Each June their sweet, citrusy fragrance fills the yard. I thank the honey locust for providing the shade, which enables them to thrive.

Once I reach the backyard, the vegetable garden is my first stop. There, in the northeast corner, beans once climbed beyond their poles and tomatoes erupted from the soil, overflowing their cages. I knew I should have pruned more often to keep them from growing too wild. But as long as they continued to yield, even if the beans were wildly misshapen and the bellies of tomatoes grazed the dirt, I left them be. If it ain't broke, don't fix it. I learned that from Brian. He's an auto mechanic. The thing is, though, sometimes you just get so used to living with stuff that doesn't work that you can't tell the difference.

The number of times I walk the yard each day depends on which child's current behavioral challenge I'm mulling, or which therapist we're preparing to see, or which email I've just written or received from a teacher, social worker, or one of my own students. At first, I walked the yard twice a day, once in the morning, and once in the late afternoon, after I finished teaching my classes. These days I typically walk the yard five or six times per day. This is a ritual, the closest I ever come to prayer.

**

In the center of the backyard, I have special fondness for my very first flower bed: that eight-foot oval now bursting with those original pushy purple coneflowers and a resurging silky aster. Now there are also two daylilies as well. But the crowning glory here is a deep purple clematis. I bought that clematis near the end of my first gardening season in 2002. As a soon-to-be single mother, plants were a luxury I couldn't afford. But she was on discount: $12.99 instead of $19.99, because of her weak stem and brown leaves. Somebody at the garden center had mistakenly left her in a location where she received a little too much sun, but not enough to kill the plant. "It won't flower the first year," the clerk told me apologetically. Except that she did. And every year after that—faithfully, spreading across every trellis I've fashioned for her.

If I walk further south, I reach the second oldest bed, one that I intended to sort of mirror that first coneflower-breeding oval. It's now shaded by a towering lilac bush that was just a tiny twig a decade ago. The older plants here include a lovely mix of coneflowers and some very determined pink, white, and lavender garden phlox, as well as a recently transplanted, plucky little pink peony. Maybe the peony is the alpha plant, since the coneflowers behave themselves here. A few summers ago, I doubled this second oval bed's length, extending it toward the three-season porch, and then I relocated two lily babies there. I was so proud of the transplants and their success that I celebrated by splurging on three brand new sage plants and a few filler petunias. In this second oldest oval, new plants and old ones co-exist peacefully, for now.

I move to the tree house and sit on the nearly 100-year old porch swing directly beneath, anchored to its floor. Brian brought the swing home from his family farm after his mother died. My husband's relationships are stronger to the dead than they are to the living, I think. He hung the swing from our largest, oldest tree, a maple, where I could stop and give thanks for an emerging circle of transplanted lilies of the valley growing at my feet.

[1] *Jim Gilbert, Minnesota Nature Notes*

Transhumanist

Each Diwali,
Amma would light up
Small earthen lamps
From a big one,
And ask us to place at
Everywhere we have a connection with:
The alcoves, the drain, the handpump,
The manure mound, the hay-cutting machine,
The tractor, bike, pumping set,
The tethers where we tie cattle,
And all the places and things that we own and use...

As a child,
I never understood the ritual,
It was just a fun time to do it.
But now,
When I ride the Royal Enfield two wheeler
For hundreds of kilometres,
And it doesn't betray me,
I feel a gratitude for it,
I feel a humane respect,
And adoration for it,
Now, I deeply understand
The ritual of placing earthen lamps
Everywhere and on everything we own.
Maybe that is how,
We feel for the things beyond humans.

Day Care

I know where all the ginkgo trees are
on the way to daycare I plot their locations like prayers.

Three by the museum
Six by the parking garage
Two by the Presbyterian church if I take the long way home

Which I do on grocery days to catch a glimpse of gold
amidst the shopping bags, the milk and eggs.
How can something so delicate be so brilliant?

Yesterday a heron watched from a rooftop as we made our morning dance.

Lunchbox. Water bottle.
Buckle One. Buckle Two.
Open the gate. Close the gate.

Did I pack the veggie straws?
Did I e-mail the form?
Did I tell you that I love you?

I heard the impatience in her wings as she stretched her long neck
waiting for wonder, for worship.

A Candle in the Dark: A Meditation on Ritual

Deer appear on the hill behind my house. It is early November, and the ground is burnished with fallen leaves as though the sky has come to earth for rest. The leaves pad the curves of my driveway threading into our cut of the valley over Noe Creek and bending along the woods that creep up the foothills behind the house.

It's not just the undressing trees that reveal the deer. They are drawn, coming to the broad valley meadow to fill their bellies with acorns for the winter. I look up from the kitchen sink to some brown movement at the hillcrest. I look up at this hillcrest often, finding only rhododendron, elm, and beech. Maybe I see a cardinal, or a wood thrush if it's summer. The deer – two does – with their life-size dusty bodies, their wet black eyes, make my breath catch. Inside, at the kitchen sink, I can feel their heat.

.

Even in the country, it can be too easy to become solipsistic. My head is down most days with my job and my work as a parent. Everything in my life runs as though by engine, including me. I can tell myself I need all the gas in my tank just to do the necessary things. I can do that for so long until all there is is countryside whirring by and I can see everything and nothing and none of it means much. The dark closes at my periphery and a thin road spools out ahead. I know death is at the end so I keep my head down.

.

In my early twenties I began following the Celtic wheel of the year with its eight festivals or "feast days." I don't know how I first learned about it, but I was a curious kid and knew my Southern Baptist Sunday school lessons didn't tell the whole story. Certainty always unsettled me, and my curiosity flared at the arcane. I'm sure my eternal soul was and still is a worry to my mother.

Coming to the invisible altar within myself on the feast days forms the parabola of my year. But Samhain, the season of fall turning toward winter, has a catalyzing feel. Things seem to be careening towards the bitter edge of winter. Days are short and nights are long and cold, a primitive reminder that everything dies in its time. Without intentional action and a sense of contemplativeness, us humans begin to rake our hooves against the cold earth and stare directly into the void of time with no rudder or recourse.

My Celtic ancestors knew this. The oak, ash, and yew trees were sacred. Creeks, rivers, bogs, and lakes were sites of great energetic confluence, and were also sacred. They gathered at certain trees and certain rivers and dedicated them, flames on a hillside, to the gods. Like holding water in my hands, I take what little is known about these rituals and look into them for my own reflection, for who I am as a continuation of those people who lived so many thousands of years ago.

Now that I am a mom it's logistically harder to get my mind to quiet, to orient the way I'd like for every feast day. But also I've accepted that low-key celebrations are my most natural rhythm. For many years it was just me, my husband, and our pets sitting around a fire under the stars. I suppose my Celtic ancestors would have gone all out with huge communal feasts, wine flowing, tits out. The truth is they were people, too, with work to do and children to feed. I imagine just getting a fire lit and gathering around it was as much of a high point in their rituals surrounding the festivals as it is for mine.

.

We nest in the tall grasses when the nights are warm. Berries and seed pods greet our hooves in the time of sun, and we roam to the scent of new growth. Our families are our strength. Our bodies are fed and strong to outrun the bobcat and bear and even the cougar, except when they aren't. Soon, a chill fringes the days. Leaves and fruits shrivel and fall. The light wanes and darkness waxes. We pick up our heads and disperse to find food. We make our own way in the dark until the light returns.

The altar is on the treed hill above my kitchen window. It is in the herb garden, where a coyote and I saw each other one day last year, separated by a pane of glass, some gravel and a thin planting of thyme. It is along my midmorning walk over the creek and through the dormant blueberry grove.

Ritual itself is about movement. It is a struck match in the world. It disrupts stasis and generates its own energy through interaction with the physical. With my body, I chant. The grass thins along the path I walk everyday. I can't remember who started it: me, or the deer?

I light a candle on my writing desk. It is a point along a great circle connecting many points: a candle; a walk in the woods; a cup of tea; a birthday dinner; a journal entry; a deep breath; a shower at the end of a long day; a Christmas tree.

The altar, the ritual, are liminal spaces. Just as I can cross into the world "beyond the veil" through the act of ritual, I believe that world can cross to ours. Now and then, I have felt a shoulder tap to look, see. These are moments in which I have a sense of a string being tugged to draw up the blinds, revealing the pulse underneath all that lives.

One such moment was on my regular morning drive to drop off my daughter at school. I steered, sleepy and vaguely aware of my workday ahead, along my usual route through the country roads towards town. As the car rounded a curb it has rounded hundreds of times, traffic ahead of me slowed along a busy turnoff. As though tugged, my head ticked toward the left side of the road. I saw a thickety, rolling hill constellated with yellow flowers, electrified to something just over the edge of nature. I looked and felt as though I was also being regarded, and happily so.

The writer Annie Dillard describes a similar experience in *Pilgrim at Tinker Creek*. She recounts a story about a girl who was blind from birth and had an operation which gave her eyesight. After the removal of her bandages, she was led into the garden, and saw what she called "the tree with lights in it."

Annie Dillard longed to see this tree for herself for years. Finally, one day, she saw it: "I was walking along Tinker Creek thinking of nothing at all and I saw the tree with the lights in it. I saw the backyard cedar where the mourning doves roost charged and transfigured, each cell buzzing with flame. I stood on the grass with the lights in it, grass that was wholly fire, utterly focused and utterly dreamed. It was less like seeing than like being for the first time seen, knocked breathless by a powerful glance. The flood of fire abated, but I'm still spending the power."

In practice, it may be a state of idleness, of "think of nothing at all," during a ritual activity that connects my experience with Annie Dillard's. Meditation is the formal path to this mind-cleansing. But the untethered mind during a drive or a walk is akin to an organic kind of meditation. A similar state of the mind occurs right before falling asleep. It is a focused unfocus, an unaware awareness, where the ego is taking a smoke break and consciousness can simply be.

.

Coming home on these dark evenings, my high beams catch movement on the trail up into the woods as I cross the creek. The deer are shadows this close to midwinter. They are a holy spirit, heard and felt but never seen. The bodily chant of their movements is written into the land.

We curl together in the deep grass of night. The moon silvers our fur and in our dreams we remember the tang of wildflowers on our tongues. In some of us, new life grows. We beat these paths in the woods to remember who we are. We do it to stay alive.

We smell what hunts us on the breeze: depression, acedia, apathy, death. Rituals hold up our side of the connection to something bigger, whether that something bigger is the spirit world, the universe, God, our ancestors, or all of those. We return to ritual because it is a language to the eternal. It is the concentrated glow of our existence, pulsing and pulsing in the void.

Brushing my Daughter's Hair

I cast a spell
as each knot untangles.
I brush from the ends up,
A practice her father must
be taught. She only sits still
after the bath, where
I was also casting spells:
joy, delight, protections
from the whimsy of danger
and the spirits of accidental
injuries, of slips and falls and bumps.
My daughter climbs into my lap
and sings one of my rhymes
back to me. She has been listening,
it seems, learning the incantations
while keeping an eye turned
to the television. I whisper my intentions
to the Universe. It is a massive uncaring
tangle. I whisper anyway. Gently
I slide a comb through knots.

EMILY HOCKADAY

Charm to Bring a Sibling Home Safe

One part luck, two parts guilt.
Three hairs from a tuxedo cat.
A glass of Scotch for nerves,
for sleep.

Dill and Rue
to ward off evil choices and
betrayals by friends. Incantation
of all the things you hopefully
taught them. A clear night

to see the road better, a clear
head. Stuffing from the heart
of one well worn and loved
plush animal, twisted into

a braid. A mother's love. A
sister's love. Strawberry Moon
by which to see the way.

PART II

ON RITUALS

The moments knitting our lives together aren't the most majestic or eventful. It's the normal, ignorable, forgettable, habitual rhythms and routines which make up the broad fabric of life. Like breathing, it happens without much attention on our part, we exist both aware and asleep. And life, miraculous and melancholy, goes on.

What stitches us together are the common threads of existing—little habits, ways of going through a day. I'm endlessly fascinated by how someone wakes up and begins, starts a new project, makes their coffee, goes to sleep, gets to work. How similar we are, how endlessly varied and interesting, even—maybe especially—in the mundane.

Because we're here, today: a miracle. Alive, awake, and blessedly blessedly here.

Here, the writers in this collection share their own rituals. May you find yourself in these quiet, vulnerable, everyday moments as well.

BETH BROWN ABLES

We're given our lives in 24 hour increments, doled out in spoonfuls—the months and weeks of our existence in seconds and minutes. We wake each morning to the new and unknown. Many find comfort in the rituals of waking, in greeting each new day:

I usually wake around 4AM. I like to read for an hour, and often my reading will inspire me to begin writing a piece or two. It is a delightful routine.

ZARY FEKETE

I know that all gardeners walk their yards in spring, but I tend to do this in a very ritualistic way, every morning, starting the moment snow melts enough for me to see the ground beneath.

REBECCA FREMO

I switch my phone alarm off and hit play on whichever audiobook I'm listening to. This eases me through ablutions and a few token exercises. Then I commune with my cat.

JACOB EDWARDS

In the company of writers, the ritual of words is sacramental, the places set aside for writing become sacred, even if they seem commonplace. A desk: an altar, a pen: a candle's flame:

I write poetry in my kitchen, and I write fiction on my couch.

MORGAN JOHNSON

I love writing in the early hours of the day at my desk in my bedroom.
OJO TAIYE

If I'm combating writer's block, I sit down at my desk in my office, with the lights dim, and open a blank document. I'll grab a book or books from the shelf behind me and open them at random until a line strikes a note with me, and then I'll respond to it.
EMILY HOCKADAY

Looking out my window at sunrise and sunset, and praying to an oversoul/abstract entity/my ancestors/nature.
ZEBIB K. ABRAHAM

I have . . . habits, I suppose, more than any rituals—coffee when I write in the morning, things put away where they belong, both in my flat and the office, and usually before I fall asleep I review what I think I've accomplished, however humble or even meagre, during that day; I review these things chronologically—they're the "sheep" I count to bring on drowsiness.
GALE ACUFF

Rituals needn't be tied to a physical space. Inspiration, even time itself, often must be stolen in the moment. In those pilfered in-betweens, words and thoughts must be caught by a net, grabbed by the tail, captured in the notes app on a cell phone. The habit is in the capture, the ritual in noticing.

I write in any quiet moment I can capture, most often on my phone. It is sporadic and typically inspired by some feeling or something I've experienced in nature. I often reread several times right after, then put it away to be surprised by later.
ABBY MOORE KEITH

I write randomly. I feel something pushing me from inside unless I put it on paper and after writing I don't like reading my work immediately. I feel free and liberated after finishing.

PADMANABH TRIVEDI

My best work is often scribbled on the back of a receipt, or in the notes app on my phone. I'm learning that for me, I need to be wading in the water to catch any fish, and never leave home without a pen and scrap paper.

MELINA FLOWERS

I write whenever I can, wherever I can. I have two small children and I wouldn't be a writer without them, they've opened my eyes to the wonder of the world, they also make it incredibly hard to write. I usually have a phrase or sentence or just string of words that bouncing around in my head for a few days before I get the chance to sit down and get it on paper, but once I do I feel immediate relief until I'm hit again.

MILLER VOIGT

Sights, scents, and tastes bring us memories, and the rituals and traditions found in childhood. Remembering is, in many ways, its own ritual, binding us to our past.

The taste of black licorice always reminds me of spring, because of Easter and the black jelly beans I'd eat then spit out as if just to remind myself that I still don't like them.

KERRY TRAUTMAN

Tea was our ritual for everything, it seemed to be magical. A cure all, celebratory or in times of crisis, everything was solved over a brew.

DONNA FAULKNER NÉE MILLER

I remember eating Dahi Cheeni (curd with sugar) before my examinations throughout my school years. It is thought to bring you good luck; scientifically too, it is high in nutrients and might help your energy levels. My mother wouldn't ever let me step out the door until I'd had at least a spoonful - and we did this for every single examination, all through 15 years of schooling!

VISHAAL PATHAK

Every Saturday morning, our whole family would drive into the city. My sister and I got dropped off at Chinese school, where we'd spend two hours learning Mandarin. When we left class, our dad would be back to pick us up, parked in that same spot on the lot each time. From there, we drove to the Chinese Community Center to collect my mom just as her yoga class ended. After that, we'd all eat lunch at this tiny restaurant in Chinatown. While we waited for the food, my sister and I would use scrap paper from class to play the game Whose Line from the improv comedy show *Whose Line is it Anyway?* After we were sufficiently stuffed, we'd stock up on necessities at the largest Asian grocery store in town, located at the same strip mall, before heading home.

SUSAN L. LIN

Saturday morning grocery shopping with Mama was a luxury. Hop in the cart, grab a Lunchable, and pick out a fresh bag of green grapes. We'd snack the entire time we'd shop, sometimes getting to the checkout line with an empty bag - nothing to show but the stems.

ANONYMOUS

No need for a grand gesture, the rituals of the ordinary are a tonic that lifts life out of the mundane and makes it significant, gifts us with structure. Like another rung on a ladder, a habit, a touch, something always done without explanation...these are the routines that make a person who they are.

When my wife and I say goodbye for any amount of time, we touch our foreheads. All other rituals (prepping the coffee, feeding the animals, knocking on wood, suppressing feelings of inadequacy) are reused, reduced, and recycled.

TOM HARTIG

I remember reading the same book on the day before school started for maybe five or six years in elementary/middle school. I have no idea why I did this, I just remember doing it.

VALERIE HUNTER

I don't know if it's unique, but in my family, when someone has a difficult exam or interview, we pour a glass of water behind them as they leave the house, so that everything may go smoothly.

JELENA DUNATO

Once a week I stand on my tiptoes and pull down a tub of medical supplies from my bathroom closet. I give myself an injection of medication for an autoimmune disease I inherited from my dad. It's a mindless activity, though I still dread it deeply. These days two out of my three children are joining me to do it, so it's becoming less mindless and more dreadful every time.

KATE YOUNG

And, always, ritual is found in the mystery of the thing itself:

Oh, all the interesting things I prefer to keep to myself. Ritual benefits from a bit of mystery.

RASHA ABDULHADI

INDEX OF WRITERS

Zebib K. Abraham, *4-5*

Rasha Abdulhadi, *23*

Gale Acuff, *9*

Abigail Bergey, *34*

Angelina Oberdan Brooks, *3*

Chris Andrei Cruz, *20*

Jelena Dunato, *27-30*

Jacob Edwards, *10-11*

Donna Faulkner née Miller, *8*

Zary Fekete, *24-25*

Melina Flowers, *22*

Rebecca Fremo, *35-42*

Shannon Greene, *45-48*

Tom Hartig, *14-15*

Emily Hockaday, *49, 50*

Valerie Hunter, *31*

Morgan Johnson, *1*

Abby Moore Keith, *44*

Susan L. Lin, *2*

Vishaal Pathak, *6*

Marisca Pichette, *26*

Daniel A. Rabuzzi, *32-33*

Ojo Taiye, *21*

Kerry Trautman, *7*

Padmanabh Trivedi, *43*

Miller Voigt, *12*

Madeline Wilkins, *13*

Kate Young, *16, 17*

Good Printed Things is a small batch publisher.

Our projects facilitate collaboration between writers, designers, and artists, and showcase the good that comes from the intersection of talents.

Each printed thing we make serves to remind us of the value of tangibility in an increasingly digital world.

goodprintedthings.com

www.ingramcontent.com/pod-product-compliance
Lightning Source LLC
Chambersburg PA
CBHW061211070526
44583CB00025B/3213